MAKING HISTORY

VIKINGS *and* their TRAVELS

Written by
David Salariya

Illustrated by
Nicholas Hewetson

SIMON & SCHUSTER
YOUNG BOOKS

Contents

Design David Salariya
Editor Penny Clarke
Consultant Rosalie David

First published in Italy by
Giunti Gruppo Editoriale, Firenze
under the title VERSO L'AMERICA CON I VICHINGHI

This edition first published in 1993 by
Simon & Schuster Young Books
Campus 400
Maylands Avenue
Hemel Hempstead
Herts HP2 7EZ

Reprinted in 1994

ISBN 0 7500 1347 8 (hardback)
ISBN 0 7500 1348 6 (paperback)

Printed in Italy by Giunti Industrie Grafiche

Introduction

THIS BOOK TELLS THE STORY of Eirik the Red and his family, who were great Viking explorers. It describes life in the settlement he founded in Greenland, and his sons' attempts to found a colony in North America soon after AD 1000.

The Vikings lived in Iceland, Denmark, Norway and Sweden. Many people think of them as fierce pirates and raiders, but, in fact, they were great explorers, expert boat builders, daring warriors, shrewd merchants and industrious farmers. It was only the shortage of good farmland, and overcrowding at home, that made them take to the seas in search of new lands to settle.

We know about Eirik the Red and the Vikings' way of life from a collection of stories called 'sagas'. These are stories and legends which were passed on by word of mouth from generation to generation, until they were eventually written down in the twelfth and thirteenth centuries. Different sagas tell slightly different versions of the Viking story. This book follows the sequence of events told in the Greenland Saga.

For a long time, people did not believe the sagas' stories about America, because information passed on verbally from one person to another is liable to be altered or distorted over the years. Real facts about real people and events become hard to disentangle from later additions and inventions included by poets and writers to make their stories more interesting and dramatic. However, in the 1960s, archaeologists working at a site in Canada found the remains of a Viking house. This was the first hard evidence to prove that the saga's story about Leif Eiriksson and his settlement in Vinland is based on fact. If these stories are true, the Vikings were the first Europeans to make the long and dangerous crossing of the Atlantic Ocean and they did it almost 500 years before Christopher Columbus discovered the 'New' World!

Greenland: A New Life

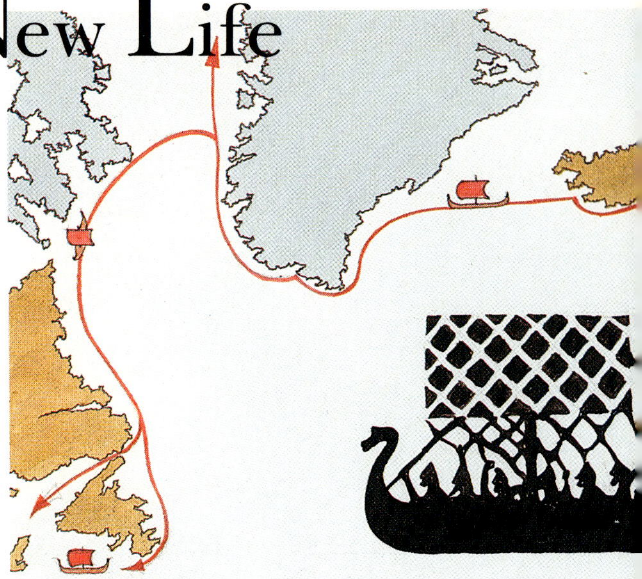

EIRIK THE RED, LEIF EIRIKSSON'S father, started the viking settlement in Greenland. In 982 he was banished from Iceland, his home, for three years because he had killed a man. Needing somewhere to live, he decided to set sail for the large island west of Iceland that had been sighted about 60 years earlier.

When Eirik reached the island he realised that it would be a good place to settle. Farm animals would survive there, as well as people, and the wild animals could be hunted for furs and walrus ivory to trade with the rest of Europe. Eirik called the island Greenland, hoping that an attractive name would encourage people to join him there.

So, probably in 986 after his punishment was over, Eirik led a party of settlers to the new land. The journey was difficult: 25 boats set out from Iceland, but only 14 reached Greenland.

When they landed, the new arrivals split up into two groups. One, lead by Eirik the Red, settled in what became known as the Eastern Settlement. Eirik's home, Brattahlid, became the island's centre of trade and government. The second, smaller, group travelled 400 miles along the coast and founded the Western Settlement.

△ The map shows the main routes the Vikings took in their journeys west to Iceland, Greenland and, finally, to Vinland (North America). The Vikings also sailed regularly around the British Isles and along the coasts of France and northern Spain. The silhouette of a sailing boat (inset) is from a Viking tombstone.

▽ Polar bear skins were a valuable export from the new colony of Greenland. Live bears were even more highly prized, but transporting one must have been difficult.

▽ Sledges were the best way to travel across the ice and snow. A beautifully carved sledge like this one was found in the Oseberg ship burial (page 17).

Farming

LIFE FOR THE SETTLERS IN Greenland was very hard. The winters were long and very cold and the summers were short.

Farming was the most important occupation, although some of the men also hunted and fished. Most of the farms were very isolated, so they had to be very self-sufficient, producing all their own food and clothes.

The summer was particularly busy for the farmers. If they did not grow enough to keep their families, servants and animals through the long winter ahead, starvation was a real possibility. Corn would not grow so far north, so farming was based on rearing cattle, sheep and a few pigs. Each summer the animals were taken to graze on the high pastures while the land around the farms was used to grow hay for winter feed. The farmers' wives grew turnips, cabbages and beans. They made cheese and kept chickens for eggs and meat.

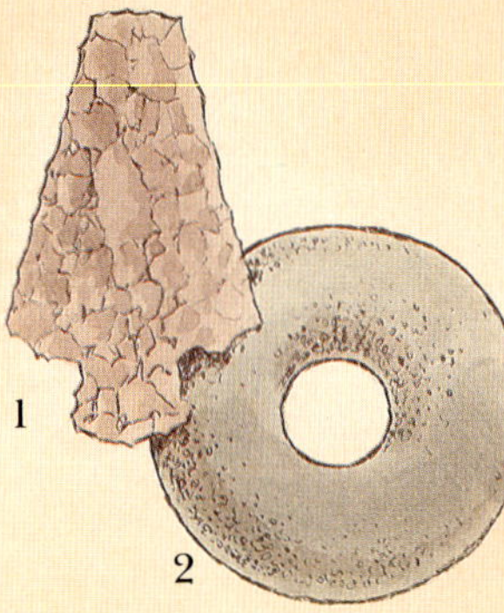

1 Arrowhead made of Labrador quartzite but found in Greenland.

2 Spindle whorl like Viking women used, from Newfoundland.

3

3 Cooking utensils from the Oseberg ship.

4 Woman at a loom and (above) ivory weaving tools.

6 Farmhouse based on one found at Stong in Iceland, which was destroyed by a volcano around 1104. The house has turf walls on stone foundations. The rooms were panelled in wood to avoid damp.

A Hall
B Living room
C Store
D Lavatory

5

5 Woman kneading bread dough.

The Vikings at Home

ALL VIKING HOMES, OR LONG-HOUSES, were built in the same way, whether they were in Greenland, Norway or Iceland. The walls were made of stone, wood and blocks of turf. In cold areas, like Greenland, the walls were extra thick. The roofs were thatched with straw, reeds or turf – it depended on what materials were available.

Inside each longhouse was a long hall. Sometimes it was the only room. The family cooked, ate and slept in it. Great cauldrons of meat stew or porridge made from imported barley hung from chains over the central hearth. There was no chimney. The smoke was supposed to escape through a hole in the roof, but this did not always happen, so the room was often smokey, sooty and dark.

▷ Keeping the fire alight was a very important task. Without a fire the Vikings had no food, warmth or light and, in the long cold northern winters, that would have been disastrous.

▷ Several generations of a family lived and worked together in the single room of the longhouse, going about their tasks by the light of the fire and a few lanterns.

Eirik the Red's longhouse had several rooms because he was the most important man in Greenland. The great hall was 15 metres long and 5 metres wide. The turf walls were 3 metres thick.

At mealtimes tables were brought into the hall. The men sat on benches along the length of the hall, while the women served the food. The owner of the longhouse sat nearest to the fire! If there were any guests, the most important sat opposite him.

Although Viking society was male dominated and marriages were usually arranged by parents for their sons and daughters, women had some rights. It was they who kept the keys to the chests in which their families put their most valuable possessions. They could also divorce their husbands.

The New World

ACCORDING TO THE GREENLAND SAGA, the first man to see the new world of North America was a Viking merchant from Iceland called Bjarni Herjolfsson. His parents had gone to Greenland with Eirik the Red in 986. Some years later Bjarni decided to join them.

He set off in the summer, usually the best time to make long voyages. However, a sudden, violent storm blew his boat off-course. When the winds died down, Bjarni spotted land, but was puzzled by what he saw. People who had visited Greenland spoke of huge glaciers and great ice-cliffs. The land Bjarni saw was low-lying, with gentle hills and thick forests. He steered his boat northwards along the flat, well-wooded coast. Then he headed eastwards – out to sea. After sailing for three days Bjarni reached a land of barren, icy rocks. But even these did not fit the descriptions of Greenland, so he continued sailing east. Finally, four days later, he reached Greenland and his parents' new home.

By accident, Bjarni had discovered what we now call North America. The wooded lowlands were probably the coasts of Newfoundland and Labrador, while the barren rocky land was Baffin Island. Inspired by Bjarni's descriptions of these lands, Leif Eiriksson set out to find them.

▽ Without good ships and skilful shipbuilders the Vikings could never have made their voyages or discovered North America. The bays and beaches beside any Viking settlement were full of the sounds of men making or repairing ships.

▽ The Vikings liked to build their ships of oak because it is a very strong wood. Gradually, over the years they had to start using other woods as oak became scarce. It grows slowly and the Vikings needed many ships. Pine and ash were other woods used.

▽ Even when oak was scarce, it was used for the ship's keel. The keel is a ship's backbone and gives it strength. It also has to withstand the strain of being dragged ashore. Timber for ships was felled in winter so it could slide across ice and snow easily.

Ships and Shipbuilders

THE VIKINGS' POWER AND WEALTH was due to the skill of their shipbuilders. These men produced superb ships which could also withstand the fierce storms of what we now call the North Atlantic.

Until the last century, all that archaeologists knew about the ships was that they were wooden, had a large square sail and could be rowed. Then, in 1880, a Viking ship dating from around AD 900 was found preserved in a burial mound at Gokstad in Norway. It had been buried because the Vikings believed in a life after death and buried dead people with the things they would need in the next world.

In 1904 another, even better, ship was discovered a few miles away at Oseberg. From these ships we now know that Viking shipbuilders did not work from plans, but built ships to a traditional pattern. First they chose a long straight oak tree for the keel. This was the ship's backbone and gave a firm base to build on. The hull was made of wooden planks held in place with wooden pegs or iron nails.

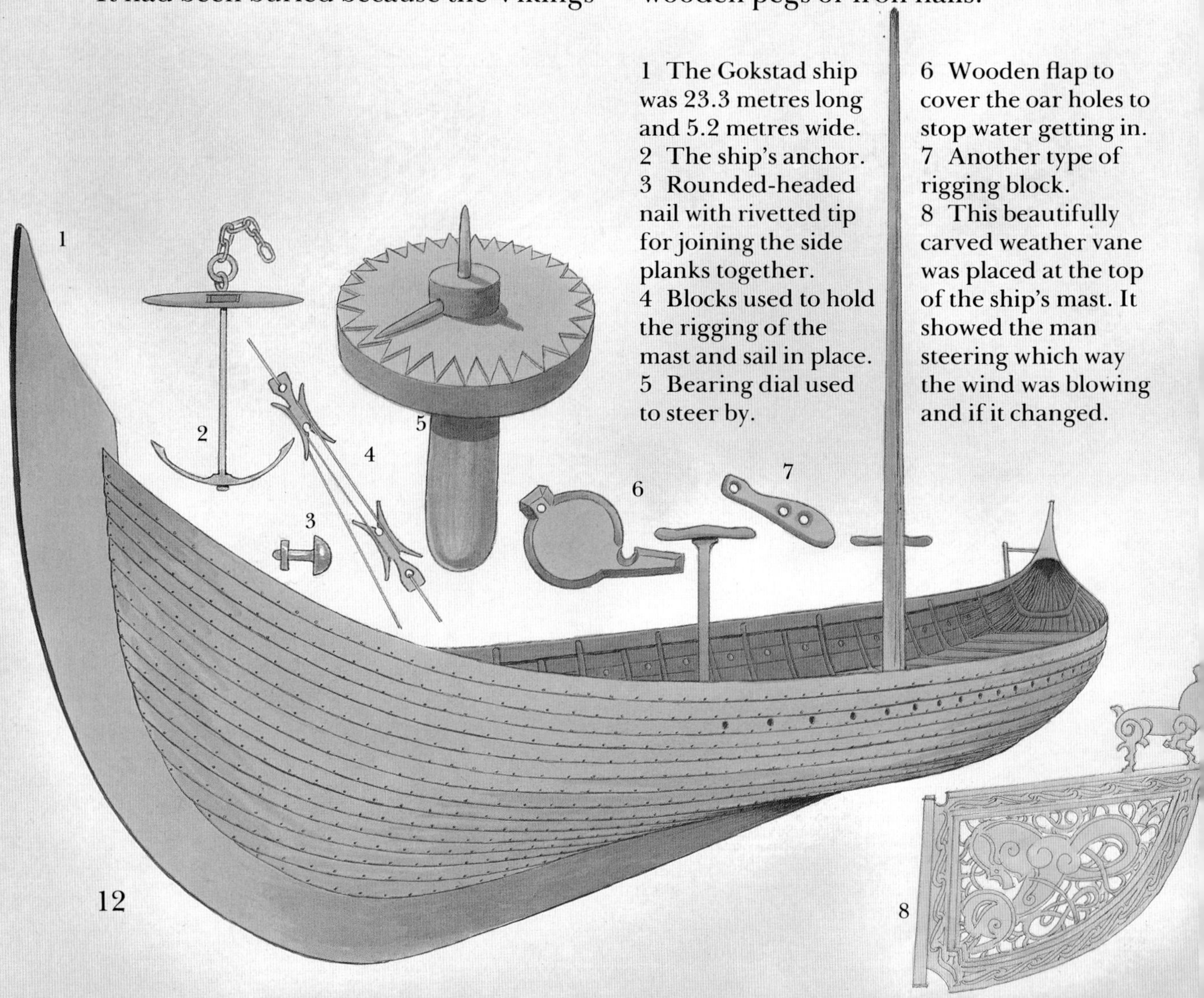

1 The Gokstad ship was 23.3 metres long and 5.2 metres wide.
2 The ship's anchor.
3 Rounded-headed nail with rivetted tip for joining the side planks together.
4 Blocks used to hold the rigging of the mast and sail in place.
5 Bearing dial used to steer by.
6 Wooden flap to cover the oar holes to stop water getting in.
7 Another type of rigging block.
8 This beautifully carved weather vane was placed at the top of the ship's mast. It showed the man steering which way the wind was blowing and if it changed.

▷ The Oseberg ship, used to bury a Viking queen, was 21.6 metres long and 5 metres wide. It was about 100 years old when it was buried.

◁ Carving of a Viking ship under sail.

▽ The letters of the Vikings' alphabet were easy to carve in wood.

9 T-shaped breast augur for drilling holes.
10 Three hammers.
11 Knife for carving.
12 Adze
13 Axe
14 Moulding irons for decorating timber.
15 Tongs for making nails.
16 Grooving chisel.
17 Detail of the carved decoration on the Oseberg ship.

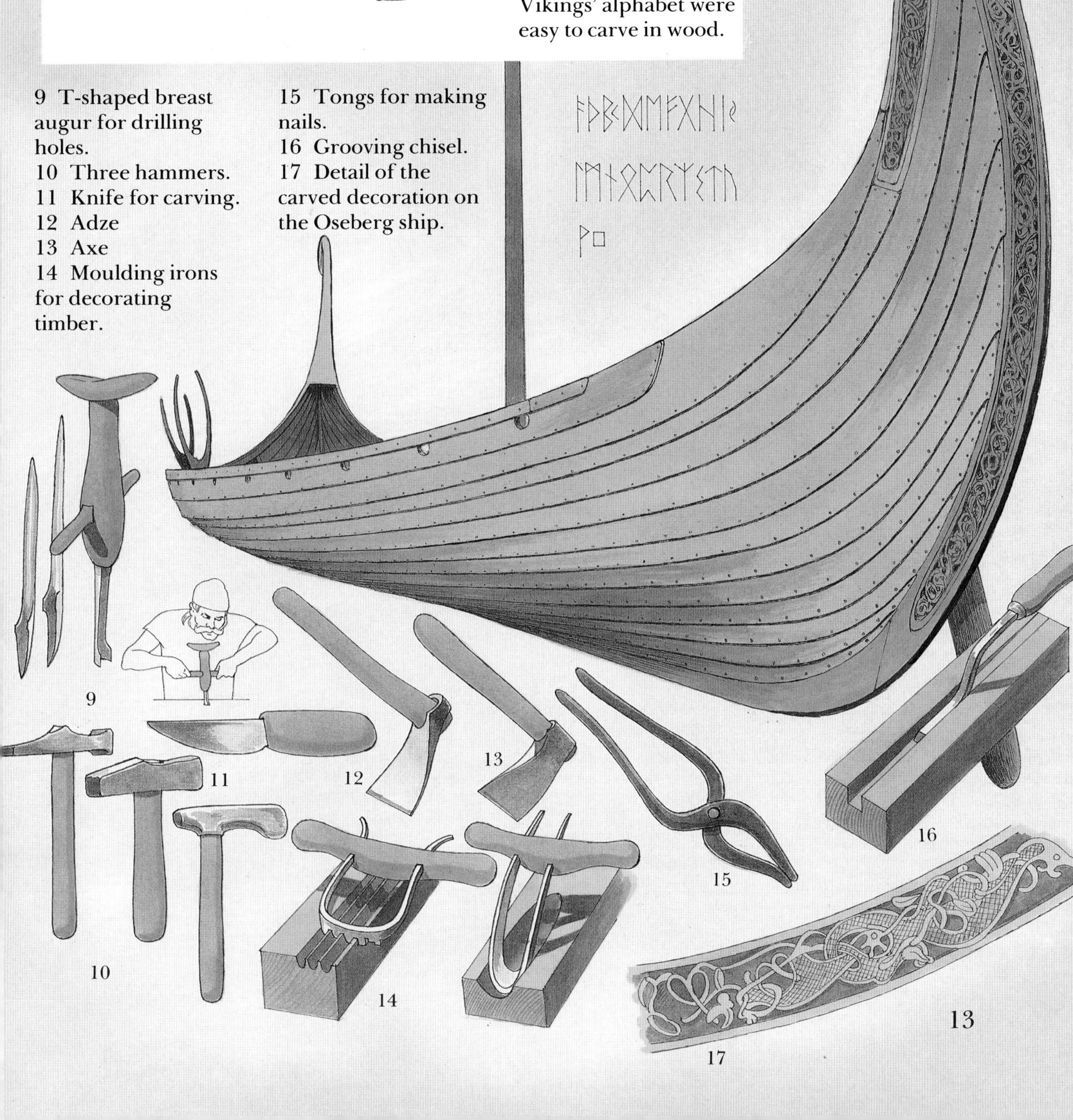

Leif's Voyage Westward

THE VIKINGS DID NOT HAVE compasses to guide them on their voyages. Instead, they usually kept close to the shore and relied on well-known landmarks to tell them their position. They knew the dangers of the open sea where, out of sight of land, it was very easy to lose all sense of direction and drift aimlessly, at the mercy of wind and tide.

When they had to sail out of sight of land, how did the Vikings find their way? They used their knowledge of the natural world. They observed the position of the sun and the stars. They also knew that warm, wet winds blew from the south-west and cold wet winds from the north-east. This knowledge was essential, because days and nights can be cloudy, without sight of sun or stars. They knew, too, the habits of migrating birds, observing that, at certain times of the year, some always headed towards land. Even so, Leif's voyage was risky.

▽ The sides of the Vikings' ships were quite low. This was fine for calm, coastal waters, but caused problems on longer voyages across rough seas. Waves breaking over the ship's sides could swamp it, so one of the crew had to spend his time bailing out the boat with a bucket.

▽ Among the seabirds that helped the Vikings locate land when they could not see it were fulmars and eider ducks. Fulmars return to the land at night, so the voyagers only had to follow them to reach the coast. Flocks of eider ducks show there is land within 100 miles.

Leif set out with a crew of 35 to find the land Bjarni had seen. He passed the barren rocky land and called it Helluland, meaning Slab-land after the shape of the rocks. He sailed onwards until he reached the flat, wooded country that Bjarni had described. This region he called Markland or Forest-land. Turning his ship southwards, he sailed on for another two days along a coast that was just as Bjarni Herjolfsson had described it, sitting round the fire in the longhouse in Greenland. The Vikings had arrived in America.

Vinland

LEIF AND HIS CREW EVENTUALLY anchored their ship in a quiet bay. Around them was low-lying fertile land with thick woods behind it. Glad their voyage was over, the Vikings soon went ashore.

They quickly noticed many differences between where they were and their home in Greenland. To begin with, the days and nights were much more equal in length than they were used to. This shows their landing place was south of Greenland, because days and nights are more equal in length the closer a place is to the equator.

The salmon in the rivers were also larger than Leif and his crew had seen before. This suggests that they had landed north of the Hudson River, because salmon are rare to the south of it.

There was plenty of timber in the woods for building houses and repairing ships. The Vikings also noticed that grass did not die back at the end of the summer as quickly as it did in Greenland, so future settlers would have to store less winter food for their cattle.

Some of the men went to explore the woods. Trykir, a German, found grape vines, which is why Leif called the place Vinland or Wine-land. Some people think the vines were really squashberry plants.

△ The forests around Leif's settlement were a good source of fresh meat and skins. The ead animals' bones could be used for tools and arrow tips.

▽ Turf was an important building material. Cut carefully, it made a strong wind and weather proof covering for the roofs and walls of houses.

Death of a Viking

THE NEXT SPRING LEIF AND his men loaded their ship with timber and skins and set sail for Greenland. There was much rejoicing when the explorers arrived safely. But the winter was harsh and many people in Greenland died, including Eirik the Red, Leif Eiriksson's father.

When spring came, Leif's brother, Thorvald, and a crew of 35 sailed for Vinland. They reached the new land safely in the spring of 1004.

Soon after they had arrived Thorvald and a small group of his men sailed westwards from the main Vinland camp. They found woods stretching down to the shore and white sandy beaches, but no humans. They spent that winter back in the camp, but, in the spring, they set off again, this time sailing east, then north along the coast.

Now, for the first time, they saw humans: nine men living in shelters made of skin-covered boats. Thorvald and his men attacked these strangers, killing eight. The man who survived summoned a much larger force to fight the Vikings. During the battle Thorvald was injured by an arrow. Realising that he was dying, he asked his men to bury him at a place he had marked as a good site for the Vikings to build a new settlement. Instead, it would become his burial place.

▽ The 'skraelings', the native Americans that the Vikings encountered, were skilful canoeists. Archaeological evidence now backs up statements in the Vikings' sagas. For example, we now know that while most tribes made their canoes out of birch bark, some preferred to use animal skins, just as the sagas describe what Thorvald and his men saw.

▽ If a man was wounded in the stomach the Vikings gave him a 'test meal'. This was a type of porridge strongly flavoured with onions and herbs. If the smell of onions came from the man's wounds, it proved that his stomach or intestines had been pierced and that he would die.

The Vikings' Assembly

EACH SUMMER THE VIKINGS HELD a meeting or assembly called a 'Thing'. In Greenland it was held near Brattahlid, the house Eirik the Red had built and where Leif now lived. The Greenlanders' assembly was based on the Icelandic 'Thingvellir' which was held every June.

The Thingvellir, or Thing, was a gathering of freemen who met to make new laws and administer the old ones. The Thing was like a law court and settled feuds about murder, divorce and land. Local assemblies could be held at any time, but the big, national Things could only be held in summer when people could travel to it. (In winter paths and tracks were blocked by snow and ice.)

The meeting of a Thing was a great social occasion. Chieftains attended it, accompanied by servants and slaves. People came not just to settle disputes, but to exchange news, arrange marriages and meet their friends.

Most Vikings had great respect for laws, which, like the sagas, were handed down by word of mouth from one generation to the next. If a criminal refused to accept the decisions made at a Thing he became an outlaw, an outcast from society and outside the protection of the law.

▽ The Vikings held their annual summer assemblies, or 'Things', out of doors in the open air, because they had no building large enough to hold every man who could attend. In summer, too, the days were long and light, so there was plenty of time for discussion and argument. Visitors who lived far away stayed with relatives while the Thing was in session.

△ Speakers took it in turn to address the assembly from a specially chosen rock. This was so that their audience could see and hear them more easily.

△ If a man did not accept the decisions made at a Thing he became an outlaw. Everything he owned could be taken from him and killing him was not a crime.

Merchants and Traders

VIKING MERCHANTS WERE WELCOME VISITORS throughout most of northern Europe. Although the Vikings had started as raiders they found that this did not provide a regular income. So, from the ninth century onwards, they set up small trading posts. Some, like Birka in Sweden, became great international ports and manufacturing centres. From Birka the Vikings opened up a network of trade routes stretching from Greenland in the west to the Caspian Sea in the east. They travelled south and east along the Russian rivers Dnieper and Volga and reached Baghdad by camel-train.

The Vikings traded furs, honey, wax, weapons and slaves for eastern spices, rich fabrics and silver. Their trade with northern Europe was in wine, glass, pottery, sword-blades and quern-stones (stones for grinding corn). Along their trade routes, the Vikings made special arrangements with local rulers. The king of the Bulgars, for example, let them build a settlement in return for one in every ten of the slaves they sold.

▽ Most merchants had a regular round of places they visited. Their visits were welcomed, not only for the goods they brought with them, but for their news of far-away places and events elsewhere in the world.

▽ The cart in the background is based on the remains of one found in a ship burial at Oseberg.

▽ The merchant is holding a pair of scales. He uses them not to weigh goods, but to weigh the silver he is given in payment for the goods he sells. The remains of similar scales made of bronze and iron have been found in the graves of merchants at the great Viking trading centre of Birka in Sweden. Some came from the Far East.

The Great Feast

IN 1008 THORFINN KARLSEFNI, a wealthy merchant, came to Greenland to trade. He stayed with Leif Eiriksson at Brattahlid, where he met Gudrid. She was a widow Leif had rescued from a shipwreck on his return from Vinland. During the winter Thorfinn and Gudrid were married and there was a great feast to celebrate their wedding.

The Vikings always celebrated festivals and family occasions with feasts. As well as plenty to eat and drink there was music and sometimes dancing too.

▽ The wedding feast of Thorfinn and Gudrid was probably like the Vikings' usual mid-winter feast, which was also a religious celebration. Meat was an important part of these feasts. It might be deer, seal, whale or bear, all the result of successful hunting trips earlier in the year. Food was eaten with the fingers and spoons.

Hospitality was important to the Vikings and generosity was admired. Living in such a harsh climate, they knew the importance of sharing food and shelter.

Poets, known as 'skalds', provided entertainment at feasts. They recited well-loved traditional stories and poems and composed new songs to praise their hosts or the guests at the feast. They might also make up a poem about a local event, mingling it with accounts of heroic deeds by gods and other mythical figures. This is how the sagas grew up and why they can vary so much.

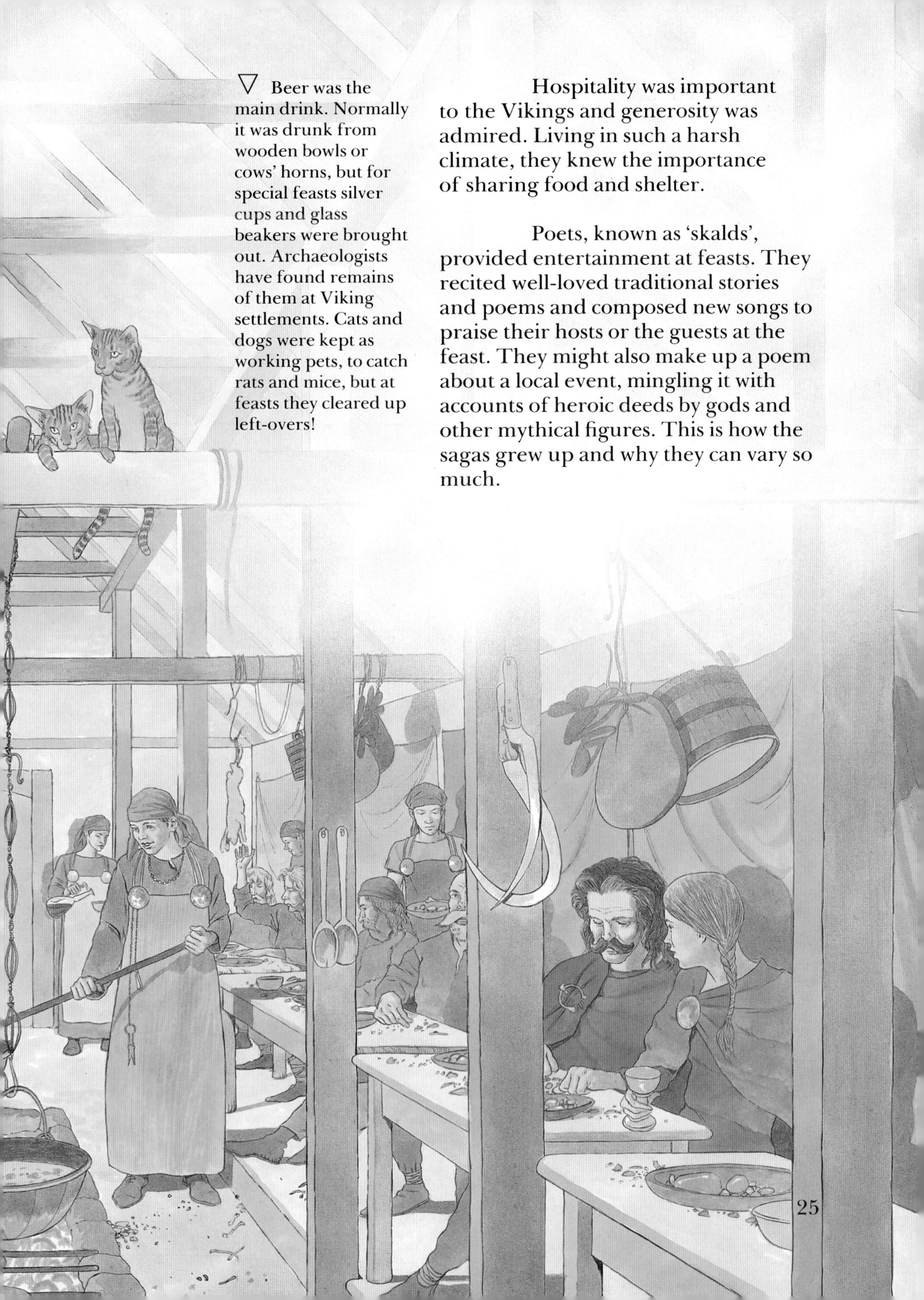

▽ Beer was the main drink. Normally it was drunk from wooden bowls or cows' horns, but for special feasts silver cups and glass beakers were brought out. Archaeologists have found remains of them at Viking settlements. Cats and dogs were kept as working pets, to catch rats and mice, but at feasts they cleared up left-overs!

Religion

△ Viking chief's funeral, reconstructed from a description written in 922.

THE EARLY VIKINGS WORSHIPPED MANY different gods and goddesses. They also had three great religious festivals: one in mid-winter, one in spring at the beginning of April and one at harvest time. At each festival they sacrificed animals to the gods, hoping, in return, the gods would give them victory in battle, good harvests and mild winters.

The Vikings believed that when a person died they went on living, but in another world. So, at Viking funerals, things the dead person had used or worn were buried too, for use in the person's new life. Although the bodies of some Vikings were cremated (burnt), many others were buried.

The Vikings came into contact with Christianity through both raiding and trading. They destroyed churches and monasteries in the north of England, taking their gold and silver treasures, often to melt down. Viking merchants certainly traded with Christian communities in the Middle East.

Gradually more and more Vikings became Christians, including Eirik the Red's wife and son, Leif Eiriksson. In 1000 the annual Thing discussed the problem. Opinions were divided about whether the Vikings should become Christians. Finally, Thorgeir, the chief spokesman, decided they should become Christians, but could still worship the old gods!

The Vikings' gods

Odin, the All Father, was the god of kings and warriors. He had two ravens as companions. Frigg was his wife.

Thor, with his hammer and great red beard, was the god of ordinary men and women. Sif was his wife.

Tyr was brave and virtuous and had once, so the Vikings believed, been the king of Heaven, but had lost his throne.

Vidarr was a rather mysterious god. Frey and Freya were the god and goddess of fertility, bringers of good crops.

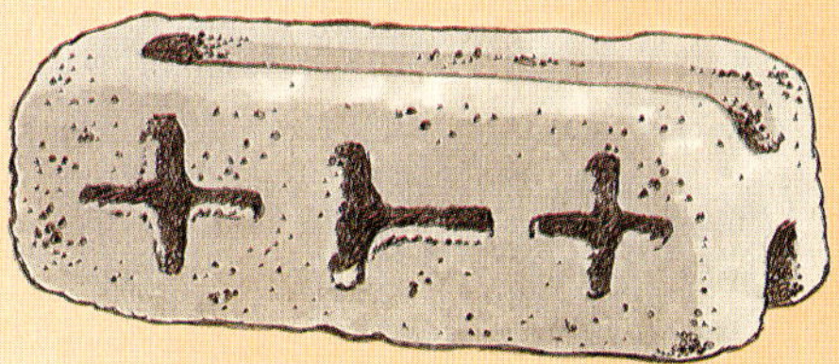

1 This mould can be used to make either Christian crosses or else the pre-Christian hammer of Thor (which is between the two crosses).
2 Silver crucifix found in Sweden.
3 Viking cross from Yorkshire, England, shows a warrior and his weapons.

1

2

3

4 The tiny church built at Brattahlid for Thjodhild, wife of Eirik the Red.

4

A New Life in Vinland

DURING THE LONG WINTER OF 1009, there was much talk in Greenland of another journey to Vinland. Gudrid, the wife of the merchant Thorfinn, was very keen to go and urged her husband to make the voyage. Thorfinn agreed and gathered a group of 65 men and 5 women willing to risk the journey.

The settlers made careful preparations for the expedition. They arranged to take different kinds of farm animals with them, as well as seeds and young plants for crops.

Thorfinn and his group set off from Greenland, probably in 1010. They reached the coast of North America safely and, following the coast, soon discovered Leif's old settlement. They continued sailing until they found a good harbour where they landed and set up camp for the winter.

They felled timber and searched for food. They found plenty for their animals, but very little for themselves. Once they were so hungry they had to eat a dead whale. It made them all very ill.

▽ Everyone setting out with Thorfinn to go to Vinland to start a new life knew they were taking a great risk. The Vikings were skilful sailors, but the voyage was long and they had no compasses or charts (sea maps) to guide them. Their ships were quite shallow and although they could ride the waves easily, for this voyage they were more heavily laden than usual, because the settlers had to take so much in the way of supplies – not to mention all the animals they needed to start their new farms.

Conditions on the voyage must have been awful. The boats were open with no protection from the weather. Although the party set out in spring, to give them as long as possible through the summer in Vinland, the weather would still have been very cold as they sailed across the north of the North Atlantic.

The End of the Colony?

THE SETTLERS SURVIVED THE FIRST winter in Vinland, but soon became discontented. Thorhall the Hunter and nine companions set out to return to Greenland. They never got there, their boat was blown off course to Ireland, where they were killed by the local people.

Thorfinn and the rest sailed south and started a new settlement. Here they met the first 'skraelings' – the Vikings' name for the native Americans.

At first the two peoples got on well, but one day the skraelings were terrified by a bull the Vikings had brought with them. (They had never seen one before.) A fight broke out and many men on both sides were killed. After this, Thorfinn decided Vinland was too dangerous. He and Gudrid returned to Greenland with their baby son Snorri – the first person from Europe to be born in North America.

The sagas suggest the Vikings' colony in Vinland survived until the twelfth century. However, by the thirteenth century, the 'mother' settlement in Greenland was declining. Colder weather, poor harvests, disease and conquest by the Norwegians forced the Vikings to abandon their settlement there. If the Greenland settlement failed, how long did the Vinland colony survive? We may never know.

▷ The new settlers' first encounters with the native Americans were peaceful and successful. Both sides were intrigued by the other. The Vikings bartered red cloth they had brought from Greenland and fresh milk for warm furs trapped by the skraelings – as the Vikings called the native Americans.

The Vikings may also have got spear- and arrow-heads from the skraelings because archaeologists working in Greenland at a place they think was the home of Eirik the Red, have found an arrow-head very like those made by the skraelings living near the Viking settlement in Vinland. And in Newfoundland, Canada, stone spindles have been discovered just like those used by Viking women for spinning!

Important Dates

The Vikings left no written records of their voyages, and the sagas are vague about when events took place, so the dates given below are, apart from the last two, approximate.

900 A ship is built that, years later, will be buried in Norway as part of a Viking's funeral. It will be discovered nearly one thousand years later.
920 First sighting by the Vikings of a large island west of Iceland.
982 Eirik the Red, banished from Iceland, decides to find the island west of Iceland. He discovers Greenland.
986 Eirik the Red leads a party of settlers from Iceland to Greenland.
990s Bjarni Herjolfsson leaves Iceland for Greenland, is blown off-course and sights North America.
1000 The Viking Assembly or Thing decides the Vikings can become Christian.
1002 Leif Eiriksson, following Bjarni Herjolfsson's directions, reaches Vinland and stays for the winter.
1003 Leif Eiriksson returns to Greenland. Death of Eirik the Red.
1004 Thorvald, Leif's brother, reaches Vinland.
1005 Vikings encounter native Americans. Thorvald is killed.
1008 The merchant Thorfinn Karlsefni marries the widow Gudrid.
1010 Thorfinn and Gudrid lead a party of settlers to Vinland.
1011 After disputes with the native Americans, Thorfinn and Gudrid return to Greenland.
1880 Archaeologists discover the Gokstad ship in Norway.
1904 The Oseberg ship is discovered a few miles away.

Index